TEACHERS RESOURCES

VICTORIAN BRITAIN

GINN
History

Contents

Introduction

The structure of *Ginn History*

Ginn History is a programme of work that offers a clear and continuous approach for the whole of the primary age range. It offers practical advice and resources for all areas of National Curriculum History. To resource the core study unit 'Victorian Britain', *Ginn History* provides the following resources:

At Key Stage 1

The Key Stage 1 *Ginn History* stories *Orphan Mary, Princess Victoria* and *Mary Seacole*, and the read-aloud stories on pages 94–99 in the *Ginn History* Key Stage 1 *Teachers' Resource Book*, will give children background knowledge of some of the personalities and events they will encounter in this study unit. The corresponding pictures in the Key Stage 1 *Group Discussion Book* will also introduce children to evidence from this period.

At Key Stage 2

The Key Stage 2 *Teachers' Handbook* provides complete support for the implementation of National Curriculum History, including guidance on curriculum planning, and full assessment and evaluation support. The *Teachers' Handbook* also contains guidance on how to teach the supplementary study units and how these units could be linked with 'Victorian Britain'.

The *Victorian Britain Pupils' Book* contains full coverage of National Curriculum content areas, specifically written with the attainment targets in mind.

The *Ginn History Victorian Britain Group Discussion Book* is an ideal focus for discussion about the Victorian period. It is directly linked to the content areas of the *Victorian Britain Pupils' Book*, and it enables children to look more closely at evidence, and to investigate further source material.

The *Victorian Britain Teachers' Resource Book* is designed to support the *Pupils' Book* by providing:

- factual background information for each spread;
- suggested activities for each spread to introduce and develop historical skills and understanding, and to link to other curriculum areas;
- photocopiable *Blackline Master* activity sheets which help develop specific skills and act as a record of assessment;
- suggestions for covering the supplementary study unit on local history through the study of 'Victorian Britain', including a scheme of work and guidance on the resources;
- further references;
- a list of key 'Victorian Britain' events.

The *Pupils' Book*

The *Victorian Britain Pupils' Book* looks closely at people of different levels of society, and at the way in which they were affected by the tremendous scientific, technological and political changes during the 19th century.

The materials in the book will prove useful for some of the supplementary study units from list A of the National Curriculum programmes of study. For example:

- Houses and places of worship are a feature of much of the book, particularly the sections on buildings and towns on pages 4–7 and 10–11, and religion on pages 40–41. Other pages such as 12–15 and 26–27 also have contributions.

- Writing and printing will benefit by including the section on schools on pages 20–21.
- Land transport should include sections on the railways, coaching and town transport from pages 30–33.
- Domestic life, families and childhood should include sections on housing, family life, children at work and at school, toys, country life, the role of women and the Victorian Sunday (pages 10–25 and 40–41).

Links with local history

In most areas 'Victorian Britain' is an ideal vehicle for local studies and so this *Resource Book* contains a section specifically devoted to that on pages 24–26.

Attainment target links

Some attainment targets have been given in detail (e.g. **En 3/2d**) whilst others have been left more open (e.g. **Te 2**) because the nature of the activity means that children may respond at a variety of levels. Where **En 3** has been identified, teachers will also have the opportunity to assess **En 4** and **En 5** if they wish. **En 1** has not been identified at every discussion point.

Pupils' Book notes

Introduction

Background information

Queen Victoria

Victoria was born on the 24th May 1819. At that time many people despised the monarchy, having had to put up with George III and George IV. Thanks to Prince Albert, Victoria managed to get on with her prime ministers, and Victoria and Albert had some influence on the political life of the country. After Albert's early death Victoria retired from public life, spending much time at Osborne House on the Isle of Wight. However, Disraeli was able to persuade her to take a more active part in the life of the nation.

Prince Albert

Victoria and Albert married in 1840. Albert was a German which initially made him unpopular with many people but his untiring work for Britain soon changed that view. He could not be called King so he was known as the Prince Consort. Albert had an excellent education and was able to help Victoria understand politics. He also had a great interest in science and technology. The Great Exhibition of 1851 was his brain-child. He worked unceasingly to make it a success. He died in 1861 from typhoid fever when he was only 42.

Times of change

Few periods in history have seen so many changes as the Victorian age. When Victoria came to the throne Britain was largely a rural country ruled by the landed aristocracy. When she died in 1901 most people lived and worked in towns, the middle class was firmly established, all men had the right to vote, all children had the right to an education, and new technology had changed patterns of life dramatically. It was a time of enormous wealth and progress for many; it was also a time of great hardship for others. New machines and low-paid workers made goods that transformed Britain into the world's leading industrial nation.

Looking at evidence

As the last spread in the *Pupils' Book* reminds us, there is evidence of the Victorian impact all around us. The postal service was largely a Victorian invention. Rowland Hill introduced the postal service, the penny black stamp and the first post boxes. The penny black stamp was first issued on 6th May 1840.

Discussion and activities

- A time line should be made on a large display board, to help the children realise the length of the Victorian period and the changes that happened during it. Each decade could have a different-coloured background and there should be ample space for children's work to be added as the theme progresses. **Hi 1/4c**
- Start making a collection of Victorian 'artefacts'. Many families have things they will lend; you could also contact your local museum, and add some works by Dickens and other Victorian writers.

Victorian towns

Background information

In 1801 about seven out of ten people lived in the country; by 1901 this number was reduced to two out of ten. Factories and mills were built in many cities, and cheap housing was built close to them to house the workforce. When Victoria came to the throne there were only five cities with a population of 100,000 or more; by 1891 there were 23. There were great changes to the towns and cities themselves during the Victorian period, most notably an expansion at the outskirts and a declining population in the centre.

By the end of the period towns like Brighton were commuter centres for wealthy businessmen who worked in London.

Manchester

Manchester in many ways was typical of Victorian cities. From a population of 80,000 at the start of the century it had grown to 142,000 by 1832. Manchester was not made a town until 1838 so there was no control on planning before that time. Private investors built what they could where they could, and all this was in the shadow of the cotton mills. Many people admired these growing towns but others recognised their problems. In 1861 a Frenchman called Taine visited Manchester and wrote: '. . . it is still more dismal. The air and the soil appear charged with fog and soot. Manufactories with their blackened bricks, their naked fronts, their windows destitute of shutters, and resembling huge and cheap penitentiaries.'

Engels was another visitor and he wrote of Manchester: '. . . dirt and revolting filth – without qualification the most horrible dwelling I have until now beheld.' However, in 1844 Disraeli wrote that 'Manchester is the most wonderful city of modern times. It is the philosopher alone who can conceive the grandeur of Manchester and the immensity of its future.' Several public buildings such as the town hall were built. These are typical of the great public buildings of the period.

Wealthier developments

Some parts of the cities were much grander than others. These 'grand' areas were sometimes in the centre but gradually during the century the suburbs developed. The wealthiest people tended to live to the west of industrial towns so that the prevailing winds would blow away city smogs and smells. The wealthier people often lived on higher ground too, since that was often better drained and above the worst of the smoke.

Discussion and activities

- Try to acquire some population figures for your town from the local history library or record office, and let the children represent these graphically. Maps might show how much your town or city expanded. **Ma 1/3c, 5/3b**
- BLM 1 – Looking at descriptions of Manchester in Victorian times. **Hi 2, 3/4**

6/7

The city slums

Background information

Poorly-paid workers crowded into small, insanitary homes. They could often only afford the rent for a room or two. There were no laws in the early part of Victoria's reign to govern the development of the towns. Piped water and toilets were rare, whole streets or courts often sharing a few meagre facilities.

The Victorians inherited many problems, adding to these in the early period, but gradually they tried to put things right, through the zeal of reformers like Edwin Chadwick who did much to reform public health.

Street children

Parents could not afford to look after large numbers of children, and many youngsters were turned out onto the streets to fend for themselves. Others were orphaned with no relatives able to care for them. *Oliver Twist* by Charles Dickens is a well-known story that highlights the problems some children faced. Many orphans joined gangs run by criminals.

Reformers

A number of people tried to change conditions for the poorest people. William Booth founded the Salvation Army, which as well as being an evangelical organisation provided food, clothing and jobs for the poor. Octavia Hill tried to provide good housing at fair rents, as long as the tenants tried to help themselves. Henry Mayhew was a journalist who wrote about the conditions of the poor and their housing. Others like Seebohm Rowntree and Titus Salt tried to improve the living conditions of their employees, and Rowntree went on to survey the city of York in 1899/1900. Dickens himself did much to bring the appalling conditions of the slums to the nation's attention.

Barnardo

Dr Barnardo was shocked to discover the number of street children in London, and he set about trying to house them. He described how in 1866 he met a boy called Jim Jarvis. It was a meeting that changed his life:

– Please sir, let me stop.
– Stop! What for? You ought to go home at once. Your mother will wonder what keeps you out so late.
– I ain't got no mother.
– But your father, where is he?
– I ain't got no father.
– Stuff and nonsense, boy. Don't tell me such stories! Where do you live? And where are your friends?
– Ain't got no friends. Don't live nowhere.
– Where did you sleep last night?
– Down in Whitechapel, along of the 'ay Market, in one of them carts filled with 'ay.
– Are there other boys like you in London?
– Oh yes, sir, lots – 'eaps on 'em.

Barnardo gave him a hot drink and some money and was taken to see the other homeless boys. He was so upset that he gave up his studies and founded a home for homeless boys in the East End of London in 1870. In 1875 he opened a home for homeless girls.

Discussion and activities

- Pictorial representations of city slums could be made using pastels, perhaps on grey paper. **Ar**
- Children could turn the Barnardo-Jarvis conversation into a play. They could then add parts to show what might happen when Barnardo tells his friends about his discovery. **En 1**
- Children could conduct a water survey. They should keep a record of every occasion in a day that they use water, perhaps classifying it into different categories. This should form a discussion focus to compare with slum dwellers in Victorian times. **Ma 5/4b, 5b**
- BLM 2 – Comparing the water supplies in slum streets with modern supplies.

8/9

Shops and shopping

Background information

Shops

Most shops were simply the downstairs room of a house. Indeed in parts of London cellars were used as shops. These shops tended to specialise in a small range of goods. Outside there would often be signs to let the illiterate population know what was sold inside. Chemists, for instance, displayed huge bottles (carboys) of coloured liquid in their window.

Many everyday items like bread and meat were delivered to middle-class homes.

Street traders

Street traders lived a very hand-to-mouth existence. They toured the poorer parts of the town or city centres. A ham-sandwich seller told Henry Mayhew that he made 3 shillings and 6 pence a week, and that 2 shillings went on rent. He often walked great distances to buy ham more cheaply.

Chain stores

Many of the larger chain stores of today were started in Victorian times. Marks and Spencer started out as a penny stall on Leeds market. Boots the Chemist started as a small shop in Nottingham, and the growth of W H Smith was closely linked to the expansion of the railways.

Discussion and activities

- Where would children go today to get the goods sold in these Victorian shops?

Baker	Stationer	Cabinet maker
China dealer	Grocer	Tea dealer
Draper	Saddler	Tallow chandler

  Do they think they would need all these things today? (Remember, these would have been common shops in Victorian times.) **Hi 1/2c, 3a; Gg 4/2c**
- Children could make up cries for street traders. There are some good examples in the musical *Oliver*. **En 1**
- Children could set up a shop in the classroom using shillings and pence (12 pence to the shilling, 20 shillings to the pound). **Hi 1**
- Discuss the pictures of Victorian shops, advertisements and packaging on pages 2 and 3 in the *Victorian Britain Group Discussion Book*.

10/11

Victorian houses

Background information

Houses for the poor

Many of the houses for factory workers that Victorians inherited were appalling. In the early part of the reign there was continued pressure to build cheaply and *en masse*. Few of these early houses exist now – many were demolished for railways to be built, while others were replaced with better housing by benefactors like George Peabody. In London some Peabody buildings are still in use. Gradually the typical dwelling became the small terraced house, sometimes with a small back yard and sometimes actually joining onto the back of another house. some of these 'back-to-backs' can still be seen, particularly in northern industrial towns. From the late 1840s onwards local authorities were established and they had a much greater say in planning and in the provision of water and sanitation.

When Dr James Kay looked into the town life of the poor in Manchester, just before Victoria came to the throne, he reported: 'The greatest portion of those districts lived in by the labouring population (mill workers) are newly built. The houses are newly built. The houses are ill drained, often ill ventilated, unprovided with toilets, and in consequence the streets, which are narrow, unpaved and worn into deep ruts, become the common resting place of mud, refuse and disgusting rubbish. In Parliament Street there is only one toilet for 380 inhabitants, which is placed in a narrow passage, from where its flow of muck infests the close-by houses. . . .'

Houses for the rich

There are many fine examples of larger Victorian houses still standing. Some of these were town houses for the landed gentry, and others were the homes of industrialists and successful men of commerce. There were many large rooms, each with a specific purpose. The scullery was a 'back kitchen' often used for washing up. The drawing room was one to which the ladies of the house and their visitors could withdraw to be alone, perhaps after dinner. The pantry was essentially a food store – the butler's or housemaid's pantry was the store for plates, table linen, etc. The gentleman of the house would probably have his own quiet room, usually the study.

There were many houses in between these extremes, in which the middle classes lived.

Discussion and activities

- Children should use the evidence from pages 10/11, and perhaps from looking at plans of local houses, to model Victorian houses. **Hi 3/3, 3/4; Te**
- This spread might give the children an opportunity to think about their own dream room. They can then design and model it. **Te**
- Read the children the whole comment by Kay, and ask them to compare it with the artist's picture of slum streets on pages 6/7 of the *Pupils' Book*. Do they think the picture is reasonable? Could they do their own? **Hi 2/4, 3/3**
- BLM 6 – Comparing rich and poor Victorian homes with the children's homes. **Hi 1/2c, 3a**

=== 12/13 ===

Rich families

Background information

'Rich' is a term used here to denote all those families who owned their own homes and had servants. It could include the landed gentry who might own more than one house, large-scale industrialists and men of commerce like bankers, but would also include many less wealthy families. In the book *The Diary of a Nobody*, for instance, Charles Pooter tells us that even with his modest six-roomed house he and his wife are able to afford a servant for general duties. Broadly this spread is about the upper and middle classes.

The roles depicted for the remote father figure and his wife who ran the household through the servants' hard work, is stereotypical but no less accurate for that.

Inside the home

Given that every room would need a coal fire in the winter, that standards of cleanliness were not as high as today, and that the Victorians did not have any of our technological cleaning equipment, it is not surprising that the décor tended to be dark. Furniture was solid and well made – the existence of so much Victorian furniture today attests to that! It too was dark. Add to this poor gas lighting compared with our modern standards and we would find the Victorian family home a fairly gloomy place.

Servants

There was much heavy domestic work: coal and hot water had to be carried to every room, even upstairs; carpets had to be taken up and beaten clean; brasswork had to be polished constantly; the laundry had to be done by hand or sent out to a washerwoman or the public laundry. It is not surprising that those who could afford it paid servants to do this work.

The servants' day was long and tiring. They would have to be up before the family and would often be the last to bed. In a large household there might be a butler, cook and parlourmaid as well as all their assistants (under-butler, kitchenmaid, under-parlourmaid, etc.). Above these socially there might be a governess or a tutor.

Many of the servants lived in the house, in small attic or basement rooms. In big houses they might even have their own flight of stairs to keep them separate from the family. Most were unmarried women who had to leave service if they wanted to marry and have children. Many started life in service as early as 14 or 15 years old.

At the end of the century a woman in service might earn as much as £50 a year, girls £28.

Parents often punished children severely if they were rude to the servants because servants were not allowed to answer back.

Looking at evidence

This is a description of a servant's attic room given in the story *A Little Princess* by Frances Hodgson Burnett: 'The room had a slanting roof and was whitewashed. The whitewash was dingy and had fallen off in places. There was a rusty grate, an old iron bedstead, and a hard bed covered with a faded coverlet. Some pieces of furniture too much worn to be used downstairs had been sent up. Under the skylight in the roof, which showed nothing but an oblong piece of dull grey sky, there stood an old and battered footstool.'

Discussion and activities

- Role play household life. Have a large household so that there can be more servants, including outside servants like the gardener and the groom. **En 1**

- Many servants came from country families. Ask the children to write a letter home describing their life. **Hi 3/3; En 3**
- Discuss with the children why people wanted to be servants, and the advantages and disadvantages of being in service. **Hi 1/2b, 3b, 4b**
- Discuss the reconstructions of Victorian rooms on pages 6 and 7 in the *Victorian Britain Group Discussion Book*.
- BLM 3 – Describing the roles of different servants.

14/15

Poor families

Background information

Skilled workers might be able to buy their own home, but they and unskilled workers were more likely to rent, especially at the beginning of the period. Various surveys were made about the plight of the poor during Victoria's reign. Perhaps the most famous is Rowntree's survey of York 1899/1900; he found that about a quarter of the people were living in poverty.

The children's wages were often vital to these families and even when laws were passed to stop child labour some parents lied about the age of their children so that they could work.

A number of shops existed for the poor. These included second-hand clothes shops where clothes could be bought and sold, and the pawnbroker's shop. As the week progressed, families often found themselves short of money. Temporary unemployment would also cause severe financial problems. One way of raising money was to 'pawn' items of value. Pawnbrokers would give a small amount of cash for clothing in good condition, or jewellery or even furniture. The family could redeem this later for that sum of money and a fee. If they did not collect the pawned item in the set time, the pawnbroker could sell it.

An urban semi-skilled worker in 1841 might earn 15 shillings a week: 2/6d (2 shillings and 6 pence) might go on rent; 3/6d on bread; 9d or 10d on coal; potatoes for the week might cost 1/4d; tea and sugar 1/6d; butter 9d. If children went to a school that would also cost a few pence. The other biggest area of expense was beer and meat which would swallow up the rest of the earnings.

Many families were much poorer than this and could only afford to rent a room or two, or would rent a house and then let out rooms in it. This overcrowding was highlighted in the Report of Common Lodging Houses of 1855. One room in Wild Court, London, housed seven people – one bed sleeping a man, three teenage daughters and their brother, the other bed their lodgers, a man and his wife. So much for privacy!

Home for many was no more than a convenient place to sleep. Children spent much of their day on the street. Parents were probably working for most of the day and then went to the pub for warmth and drink. Often the home was a workshop in which the wife and children tried to increase the family's earning power. Many manufacturers sent work out to these homes and paid very low rates for a set number of finished items.

The workhouse

Some of these conditions might seem appalling to us, but they were better than the alternative – the workhouse. Each workhouse served a particular area and was supported by local rates. So that only the genuinely needy would apply for relief, conditions were deliberately made unpleasant. When they entered a workhouse a family was split up, men, women and children being housed in different parts. Paupers, the inmates of the workhouse, had to wear special clothes, and they were given only small portions of food consisting of gruel, bread and a little meat and cheese. In some workhouses talking at mealtimes was forbidden. The inmates had to work if they were fit enough – it was boring and unpleasant work: rock breaking, oakum picking (unravelling old rope), corn grinding or bone crushing. Pauper children could be apprenticed to employers such as sweeps. In *Oliver Twist* there is a good description of a workhouse.

Looking at evidence

Rowntree wrote this about the diet of the poor: 'The food of these people is totally inadequate, consisting largely of bread, dripping and tea; bacon, bread and coffee with only a little butcher's meat.' And this about the use of pawn shops: 'The pawn shop often plays an important part in the lives of the people in the slums. The children are sent off with a weekly bundle and a number of them may sometimes be seen sitting on the steps waiting for it to open. Some families pawn their Sunday clothes every Monday and redeem them as regularly on the following Saturday night when the week's wages have been received.'

This is what a young boy said about his workhouse food in 1840: 'I was hungry, but that bread! That greasy water! Those few lumps of something which would have made a tiger's teeth ache to break the fibres of. The strangeness and foulness made my heart turn over, and I passed what I could not eat to those near me, who ate all I could spare.'

Discussion and activities

- Ask the children to make a display based on the evidence in the *Pupils' Book* and the extracts from Rowntree. **Hi 1/4c, 3/3, 4**

- Ask the children if they can bring in a week's shopping bill (perhaps the till roll from the supermarket) and compare this with the expenses of the Victorian family (listed on page 9).   **Hi 1/3a**
- Read the children the evidence about workhouse food, and extracts from *Oliver Twist* concerning the workhouse. Get them to write a letter to the local Workhouse Board suggesting some improvements. Ask them why they think the Victorians did not make these improvements.
      En 3; Hi 1/3b, 3/3, 4, 4b
- Discuss the pictures on pages 8, 9 and 11 in the *Victorian Britain Group Discussion Book*.
- BLM 4 – Writing about conditions in a workhouse.

16/17

Factories and mines

Background information

The industrial revolution

Before the 19th century most goods were made by people working from their own homes or in small workshops. The invention of new spinning and weaving machines in the late 18th and early 19th centuries changed all that. These new machines were expensive compared with the tools used in the home and needed major sources of power, usually either a water wheel or steam engine. Cotton manufacturers, in particular, began to build factories to house the new machines. These factories produced cotton more cheaply than home workers and so eventually they took over the market. Many textile factories were built immediately before the Victorian period but the principles were soon applied to other goods as well.

Steam engines

Another invention of the 18th century, steam engines were increasingly harnessed for a whole range of production processes: pumping water, grinding corn, sawing wood, grinding cutlery, etc. They were used in breweries, tanneries, soap manufacturers, iron foundries, the mines, and of course in the textile mills. Unlike the people operating them the engines could keep going all day, so factory owners were keen that factory workers should work as long as possible to gain maximum benefit from the machines.

Coal power

These factories were nearly all powered by coal. There was a terrific increase in the demand for coal during the 19th century for industrial and domestic uses. Coal mines stretched across the country, and the main mining centres were the Midlands and the North of England (Yorkshire, Derbyshire, and Nottinghamshire). Mines were owned by individuals or companies who were concerned with making a profit. Hewers dug the coal out of the coal face using hand tools. They loaded it into little trucks. Drawers or hurriers then dragged these carts to the mine shaft. Sometimes the coal would have to be carried if the tunnels were not suitable for carts. Bearers would carry large amounts of coal on their backs, and this might include climbing ladders to change level. The bearers and drawers were often the wives and children of the hewers. They were all paid according to the amount of coal they produced, so could not afford to rest. In some tunnels small doors called traps would have to be opened to allow the carts through. Young children called trappers would sit by these all day long just opening and closing the trap. Large mines would have a steam engine to wind the coal and the people up the shaft, but in small mines this winding was done by hand.

Victorian reforms

The Victorians inherited many of the worst aspects of factory and mine life but gradually the period saw a number of changes as reformers got Parliament to regulate industry. In 1842 the Mines Act made it illegal to employ children under 10, in the mines, and a proper system of inspections was set up. In 1844 the Factory Act restricted children aged 8–13 to $6\frac{1}{2}$ hours of work a day, either in the morning or the afternoon. The 1847 Factory Act only allowed women, and children under 18, to work a 10-hour day. There were still many industries not under the control of the Factory Acts so in 1867 most industries were brought under the control of the Acts. In 1878 the Acts were extended to small workshops and to workers at home.

Looking at evidence

We know about the conditions in the mines thanks to a government commission that reported in 1842. A girl called Betty Harris told the commission: 'I have a belt round my waist, and a chain passing between my legs, and I go on my hands and feet. The road is very steep. The pit is very wet where I work; my clothes are wet through almost all day long.'

An eight-year-old trapper's day was recorded as follows: 'Between two and three in the morning his mother shakes him. He fills his tin bottle with coffee, and takes a loaf of bread and sets out for the pit. All his work is to open the door and then allow the door to shut itself. He sits alone and has no one to talk to. He has no light. By five o'clock he may get home.'

Discussion and activities

- Read the extracts and ask the children to look for other evidence of conditions in the factories and mines in the *Pupils' Book*. They could then make a small poster or similar illustration entitled 'Conditions in the mines/factories'. **Hi 1/4c, 3/3, 4**
- Help the children to realise just how hard the work was: either ask them to do some boring repetitive activity for a period of time, or ask them to move a heavy box of books for a distance, and back again. They need to be reminded that workers did this all day, every day.
- Examine closely the picture showing the factory interior. Explain that the large bands are concerned with the transfer of energy from the steam engine to the workers' machines. Ask the children to devise a system to transfer energy – pulleys and cogs are both good examples. **Te; Sc 4/4b**
- If any of the children have a working model of a steam engine, ask them to bring it in to show the class.
- Look at the picture on page 10 in the *Victorian Britain Group Discussion Book*.

18/19
Children at work

Background information

Climbing boys

To keep the chimneys of large houses clean the Victorian sweep would get young boys to climb up inside them. These chimneys might be as small as 30 cm square. The boys would knock the soot down. A climbing boy's career would last until he was about 14 and then he would be too big. The work was dangerous and painful. The boys' knees and elbows were rubbed raw and sweeps would treat the grazes with brine – this was supposed to harden the skin. Many children were afraid to climb, as it was dark and suffocating. Climbing boys were often sold to sweeps by desperate parents or apprenticed from the workhouse. Their masters would encourage them by sticking pins in their feet or even lighting a fire beneath them! Lung cancer was a common killer. Lord Shaftesbury did much to improve the lot of child workers.

Mill workers

In the textile mills children worked 12 hours a day and might work up to 16 hours in busy periods. Meal breaks were infrequent and usually only half an hour long. Any child working slowly or falling asleep on the job could be beaten (strapped). The heat, dust and noise made many children ill. Many were seriously injured as they cleaned working machines that were unfenced.

Brickyards and potteries

In the brickyards children were used to carry clay. Large weights of clay were carried on their heads. At nine some children carried as much as 40 pounds' weight on their heads, or perhaps bricks would need moving in the same way. Sometimes children were so tired that they could not return to work the following day. For this labour they might get 2½ pence.

Home workers

Many children worked alongside their parents at home. An activity like matchbox making might earn 3 pence for a thousand boxes. This was hard, boring work and was not covered by the Factory Acts.

Match girls

Some children made matches. This was very unhealthy work. Bundles of matches had to be dipped into phosphorus and glue. The phosphorus caused a disease called necrosis of the jaw ('the flute', according to the girls) – the gums and face would swell and gradually the teeth would fall out. Later, parts of the jawbone would fall off. The children might work a 10-hour day in winter and 13 hours in summer. A female editor called Annie Beasant was appalled when she heard of the conditions of the match girls, and published their problems in a socialist paper called *The Link*. Eventually the match girls at the Bryant and May factory in the East End of London went on strike (1888) and won better conditions.

Street children

Large numbers of dirty ragged children could be seen on the streets of Victorian cities. Many lived by begging, others by selling flowers, cress, or matches. In London some earned a living sifting through the mud of the River Thames at low tide.

Shaftesbury and the reformers

Many people tried to improve the lot of children and other workers. The most famous individual is Lord Shaftesbury. He was responsible for the setting up of the Children's Employment Commission which reported in 1842. He was also responsible for the 1842 Mines Act, forbidding the employment of children under 10 in mines. He continued to crusade until his death in 1885.

Looking at evidence

In 1863 William Wood told the Children's Employment Commission: 'In a prosecution at Stalybridge not very long ago it was proved that two boys had swept seventy-eight chimneys in three days for the prisoner (the sweep). When he was called upon for his defence he said to the chairman, "You know my lad sweeps your chimney."

Mr Beach remembered: 'two nice little boys, aged nine and eleven, where I was apprenticed, being sold one Sunday morning for £1 10/- the two.'

Discussion and activities

- Read the evidence above to the children and get them to talk about the conditions of climbing boys and other children. Why did many Victorians, like the judge above, continue to have boys clean their chimneys even though it was against the law? Why did parents allow their children to do jobs like this that could kill them?   **En 1; Hi 1/2b, 3b, 4b, 5b**
- Ask the children to begin a booklet on children in Victorian times. It should include information on work, schools and toys.   **Hi 1/4c**
- Ask the children to make a large display of pictures with captions about Victorian childhood, using evidence in the *Pupils' Book* and from above. **Hi 1/4c**
- Ask the children to compare Victorian childhood with another period they have studied. Headings might be: work, play, clothes, schooling, care.   **Hi 1/3c**
- Discuss the pictures on page 12 in the *Victorian Britain Group Discussion Book*.
- **BLM 7** – Debating the employment of climbing boys.

20/21
Children at school

Background information

Schools for the poor

At the start of the Victorian period there was a mixture of schools catering for the poor. Whether or not children went to school depended very much on where they lived and whether their parents could afford to send them – the loss of earnings was the important factor here.

Sunday schools had been set up for a number of years. Here children learnt to read the Bible. Often the children were very tired, as they had been at work all week. Some of these church schools became weekday schools as well. The monitorial system was brought in by Joseph Lancaster – he managed 50 pupils all on his own! In the monitorial schools the teacher taught the lesson to a few selected children (monitors) who then taught the same lesson to the rest of the class. There would be rows of desks in the middle of the room and space at the side for the monitors to call out their pupils and stand them in a semi-circle and teach them.

Paper and pencils were too expensive, so old roofing slates were used instead.

For children who lived in the roughest areas of the cities there were what were called ragged schools. Lord Shaftesbury helped set up the Ragged School Union. In 15 of its schools there were 2,345 children:
162 confessed they had been in prison;
116 had run away from their homes;
170 slept in lodging houses;
253 lived by begging;
216 had no shoes or stockings;
280 had no hat;
249 had never slept in a bed.

In some areas there was no alternative to the dame school. Here children would crowd into a woman's home and be taught the basics of reading and writing.

A number of factory owners like Robert Owen and Titus Salt tried to improve conditions by building schools as part of their factories. Owen introduced the object lesson: a teacher would hold up an object such as a piece of clay, glass, a flower or a picture and would ask the children questions about it – at the time this was an innovation and brightened up the learning process.

Government intervention

Thanks to the efforts of a number of influential people the government began to help out. In 1833 the first grant of public money (£20,000) was made for building schools. Inspectors were sent to see that the money was properly spent; this helped show up the need for more government action. Colleges were set up to train teachers. Pupil teachers would start work at about 13 years old. After five years working under a trained teacher, pupil teachers could apply to a training college.

In 1861 the government asked inspectors to test pupils to determine the level of grant a school would get. This payment-by-results method was very unpopular with teachers and children. It resulted in many teachers just teaching children to pass the test.

When many more people were given the vote in 1867, Parliament decided that the electorate must be educated. The Education Act of 1870 set up School Boards to organise education in local areas. Parents usually had to pay to send children there (about two pence a week). Ten years later it was made compulsory for parents to send their children to school and in 1891 the elementary schools were made free. Lessons in these schools centred around the three Rs, using rote learning.

Grammar and public schools

Middle-class parents paid for their sons to go to grammar schools where they learnt Greek and Latin grammar. Upper-class parents could afford to send their sons to the large public schools like Rugby and Eton. Middle- and upper-class girls were usually educated at home, though some parents were enlightened enough, towards the end of the century, to send their daughters to girls' schools.

Discussion and activities

- Read extracts about school days to the children – *Nicholas Nickleby* includes a description of a private boarding school (Dotheboys Hall), D. H. Lawrence wrote about life as a pupil teacher in *The Rainbow* (1915), or you might be able to borrow or copy some school log books from the local history collection.
- Have a Victorian school day. Ask children to come in suitable clothing; set the 'desks' in rows; make children stand when you come into the room; use the rote method to learn tables; write on slates or try to use nibbed pens; have an object lesson; have a 'drill' lesson for PE; above all, be stern! Children might bring bread and cheese for their lunch.
- Using the experience from having a Victorian school day, the evidence in the *Pupils' Book* and from extracts like those mentioned above, get the children to make comparisons between Victorian schools and their own schooling.   **Hi 1/3a, 3/3**
- Discuss the pictures on pages 14 and 15 in the *Victorian Britain Group Discussion Book*.
- BLM 9 – Looking at a typical Victorian school day.
- BLM 10 – Looking at differing views about the education of girls.
- BLM 11 – Writing with pens and ink in a copybook.

22/23
Toys

Background information

The use and development of toys in Victorian England depended on two things: the increased prosperity of the middle classes which provided a bigger market; and increased technical competence which provided cheaper toys.

Nursery toys

The rocking horse was the pride of the nursery. Many were designed to take passengers. The favourite was the dapple grey. Mothers greatly approved of their daughters playing with dolls' houses as this was supposed to help them learn how to run a house properly. By the 1880s furniture for dolls' houses was being made in perfect detail. The dolls themselves were a work of art. The Victorian period was the age of the wax and china doll. Only the head was made from these materials; the body was made from calico, kid or wood and sometimes the dolls had human hair. Most dolls were dressed as adults. Some could walk, or talk. A poorer child might have a rag doll or a doll simply made from a wooden spoon or clothes peg wrapped in cloth. Other nursery favourites were building blocks, tumbling clowns and games like *Happy Families*.

In some families the only toy that could be played with on Sundays was the Noah's Ark.

Older children

The toy theatre was a popular toy with older children, especially boys. First they had to buy and perhaps construct the stage from wood and cardboard. The theatre was often lit with tiny oil-burning lamps. Sheets of characters and scenes cost a penny plain or tuppence coloured – most children preferred to colour the sheets themselves. These would be glued to card and the characters used to enact plays – scripts for these could be bought as well.

Girls would keep busy with needlework. They practised stitching by embroidering letters of the alphabet, texts or trees and flowers onto samplers.

Scientific toys were also popular – engines, the magic lantern, the zoetrope and the microscope.

Outdoor games

Balls, hoops and tops were common. Marbles came in a variety of colours and could be got from the neck of old bottles. Cricket was the 'national' game but football was gaining popularity – the Football Association was created in 1863 to standardise rules. The Rugby Union was formed at about the same time. Young ladies might participate in archery. Croquet was a popular game, as was the relatively new game of tennis. There was also a great variety of entertainment on the streets – bands and organ grinders, for instance.

Discussion and activities

- Children should participate in as many games as possible. Have a day when only hoops, tops and marbles are allowed in the playground.
- Ask the children why they think they have so many more toys than most Victorian children.
- Discuss the pictures on page 13 in the *Victorian Britain Group Discussion Book*.

24/25
Country life

Background information

Villages

Not all villages were dependent on agriculture. Some were mining or quarrying villages, others were fishing villages and others acted as dormitory villages to the big cities. Agriculture though was most important. Village craftsmen like blacksmiths, carpenters, wheelwrights, saddlers and coopers not only made many tools and household utensils but also repaired them. Most larger villages were fairly self-sufficient in this respect even after the coming of the railways.

Houses

These were often very poor. Rooms were low and narrow with small windows. They contrasted sharply with the large country houses of the landed gentry. Few labourers' cottages have survived until today.

Working on the land

The farm labourers who lived with a farmer or were employed on an estate had the most secure jobs. Other jobs were seasonal. Even after the introduction of machinery most jobs were still done by hand, though technological advances meant better hand tools were available. Many of the jobs undertaken by agricultural labourers were very skilled. In the 1880s a labourer might receive 14 or 15 shillings a week.

Depression

A series of bad years in the 1870s led to an agricultural depression. One of the chief causes was poor weather. During this time farmers got as little as a third of the normal yield from their land. Prices did not go up, though, as the shortfall was made good through imports, particularly of beef and wheat from America.

The landed gentry

Not all country life was as poor as this. For those who owned the farms and large estates life could be very pleasant. Servants and labourers did the hard work. The man of the house would often see to the management of the estate or farm; the woman of the house managed the domestic arrangements, or there might be others employed to do it. Activities like hunting and shooting were popular. On summer afternoons there might be croquet parties or walks. In the evenings there might be dinners or balls given in the neighbourhood.

Looking at evidence

In *Lark Rise to Candleford* by Flora Thompson, houses are described: 'Some of the cottages had two bedrooms, others only one, in which case it had to be divided by a screen or a curtain to accommodate parents and children. Excepting at holiday times there were no big girls to provide for, as they were often all out at service. Still it was often a tight fit, for children swarmed, eight, ten or even more in the families . . . beds and shakedowns were often so closely packed that the inmates had to climb over one bed to get to another. In nearly all the cottages there was but one room downstairs, and many of these were poor and bare, with only a table and a few chairs and stools for furniture.'

Discussion and activities

- Read the evidence from *Lark Rise to Candleford* to the children. Ask them to use this and the information in the *Pupils' Book* to make their own drawings, descriptions or models of country houses. Ask them what else they would like to know and what might help them to find out about it. **Hi 3/3, 4, 5**
- The children should take the list of the country craftsmen (under 'Villages') and decide what each actually did. Then they should decide whether we need those jobs doing today, and if so by whom. **Hi 1/3a, 4a**
- Discuss the harvest pictures on page 4 in the *Victorian Britain Group Discussion Book*.

26/27

Victorian women

Background information

Attitudes towards women depended on social class. For the middle-class man it was a sign of his economic prosperity if his wife stayed at home. It is often said that the Victorians did not approve of women working but when we consider the number of women working in all manner of jobs this is obviously not true. Throughout the period women were employed in a whole range of physically demanding work, in the factory or as servants. It was the middle-class man who did not approve of his wife working. Many women found this life unchallenging and tried to change the situation. Gradually some women like Octavia Hill led the crusade for the improvement of conditions for the poor. Others like Beatrice Webb and Phillippa Fawcett tried to get better education for girls. Gradually victories were won. After a long legal battle Elizabeth Garrett Anderson was able to become a doctor in 1870; by 1883 she was Dean of the London School of Medicine. Queens College in London was the first girls college. Miss Buss and Miss Beale were students at Queens College, and went on to establish new schools for girls. Gradually working-class girls were able to have a better education and teachers training colleges were set up. The vote was the one area in which Victorian women were able to make little progress.

Discussion and activities

- Discuss with the children the contradictions in the Victorian middle-class man's ideal of 'a woman's place is in the home' and the reality of so many working women. **En 1; Hi 2/4**

- Ask the children to write about working women as if they were either a Victorian middle-class man, an educated woman, or one of a family who needed the income. **En 3; Hi 2**

Inventions and discoveries

Background information

The 19th century saw a remarkable number of inventions. In the home candles and oil lamps were replaced first with paraffin lamps, then with gas lamps and then by the electric light; carpet beaters were replaced by carpet sweepers, wash-tubs and dollies by washing machines; coal fires by gas fires; and kitchen ranges by gas ovens. Sewing machines made possible the development of the mass clothing industry and so reduced the cost of clothes. New printing methods brought down the cost of newspapers at the same time as education reforms helped more people to read. Typewriters provided more jobs in offices, and the telephone exchanges had to be staffed – these jobs mostly went to women. Improvements were made for storing food: canned food became available after the Great Exhibition, and refrigeration meant that cheap meat could be imported from America and Australia.

Changes in health care, transport and industry are described on pages 30-33 in the *Pupils' Book*.

Many individuals helped bring about these changes, and the patronage and interest of Prince Albert helped. Faraday, Edison, Swann and others moved the industrial revolution into the home, while Darwin and others instigated an intellectual revolution. Darwin in particular was a source of controversy – many people could not reconcile his findings with the Bible, and his theory of evolution caused a considerable storm.

Discussion and activities

- Ask the children to make a list of things in their own home that a Victorian would be surprised to see, and a list of items that a Victorian would not be surprised to see. **Hi 1/3a, 4a**
- Ask the children to make an advertisement for a new Victorian product such as a refrigerator or a washing machine. **Ar; Te**
- Discuss the pictures on pages 18 and 19 in the *Victorian Britain Group Discussion Book*.

Travel and transport

Background information

Cabs

At the start of the Victorian period any form of transport except feet was too expensive for the majority of people. The wealthy used hansom cabs in the town. These two-wheeled vehicles could accommodate two passengers in a small cab drawn by one horse. The driver stood at the back of the cab and guided the horse from over the roof. In the roof there was a small hatch which enabled the passengers to talk to the driver. 'Growlers' were larger four-wheeled vehicles that were also used in towns.

Coaches

Between towns, travelling by foot, horse or coach were the early alternatives. During the Victorian period roads underwent considerable improvements, as did the coaching system. The extract on page 31 comes from *Nicholas Nickleby* by Charles Dickens and describes a journey that Nicholas takes by coach.

Buses

Horse buses were first introduced in 1829. At first they were single-deckers pulled by three horses with a driver and a conductor. By 1850 these were replaced by vehicles drawn by two horses, with a bench that ran the length of the roof, and 30 years later the upper seats were in rows across the bus. There were no bus stops as such – people hailed the buses as they would a cab. There were a number of private companies in each city and fierce competition often resulted in conductors fighting over passengers. Drivers started work at just before 8.00 a.m. and might work through until midnight. In 1851 such a driver might earn 34 shillings a week – but he would be fined if his bus was late!

Trams

Trams were first introduced in Britain in Birkenhead in 1860. They were of enormous importance because they were cheap enough for the average worker to use. Trams have been described as the 'gondolas of the people'. The widespread introduction of trams meant that cities expanded outwards as people were able to afford the daily travel to and from work. They were also able to travel to entertainments like football matches or to other public events in the parks.

Waterways

The Victorian period saw the railways take over the heavy freight trade from the canals, though in the earlier part of the 19th century the canals were very important.

Individual transport

The introduction of the bicycle as a form of transport helped 'liberate' many people from public transport. The penny farthing appeared in the 1870s but it was the introduction of the 'safety bicycle' in 1886 that made the bike a realistic form of transport for many. The introduction of the pneumatic tyre two years later helped make the bike a lot more comfortable. The first British cars were made by Lanchester but only the very rich could afford them.

Discussion and activities

- Children should draw a series of pictures to show the range of transport used in the Victorian period. Each should be accompanied by an explanation of their importance. **Hi 1/4c**
- Children should make design proposals and carry these out for a form of transport, either based on Victorian transport or transport for the future. **Te**
- BLM 13 – Constructing a transport time line.

```
┌──────────── 32/33 ────────────┐
│                                │
│         The railways           │
│                                │
└────────────────────────────────┘
```

Background information

The railways and change

The railways led to drastic changes. The 1840s saw the height of the frantic building of railways. The coming of the railways changed the lives of everyone in Britain. People could move around the country much more quickly, towns and cities developed 'commuter areas' alongside the railway development, fresh foods could be moved from distant places to the towns quickly and so still be fresh, and people were able to go on excursions to resort towns.

The building of the railways had dramatic effects on some towns. Slum areas were swept away to make way for the railway, its viaducts and its stations. The railways also divided cities up into neighbourhoods which developed an identity of their own – these still exist in some places. The suburban railways, especially in London, stretched the distance that workers could live from their workplaces, and so the boundaries of big cities exploded outwards. Cheap fares for workers were introduced in London in 1864, and in 1883 the Cheap Fares Act gave the Board of Trade power to insist on cheap workers' fares.

Some towns became important for their railway engineering works and grew rapidly: Swindon and Crewe are good examples.

There were three classes of travel for passengers: first-class passengers had well-padded seats and a roof, while those travelling third class had no seats and little room, and had to hang onto a handrail. Conditions gradually changed during the century.

The trains also improved communications. The postal service benefited greatly, as did the newspaper industry – the first daily paper, *The Telegraph*, was introduced in 1855.

Engineering feats

The opening of the Cornish Railway is a good example of the engineering feats carried out by the Victorians. The side piers of the bridge across the River Tamar are on the river banks, but the middle pier's base is 20 metres under water. The bridge is 683 metres long and from its foundations to its top it is 79 metres high. The first train across, as part of the opening ceremony, was the Royal Train carrying Prince Albert.

The hard work on the railways was done by the navvies. They tended to follow the work around the country, often living in temporary accommodation, sometimes made only from tree branches and turfs.

The Underground

In London the first section of the Underground, from Paddington to Farringdon (Metropolitan Line), was completed in 1863. By 1884 the Inner Circle was completed.

Discussion and activities

- Ask the children to take on the role of one of the following:
  - a farmer with fresh food to sell;
  - a farmer whose land is to be bought by the railway company;
  - a coach driver;
  - the owner of a coaching inn;
  - a navvy;
  - a worker living in the middle of a city who might like to move house;
  - someone who cares for the environment;
  - holidaymakers.

  Each child should write or speak in praise or otherwise of the coming of the railway. **Hi 2, 3/3**
- Get the children to demonstrate the principle of the piston. They can use a toilet-roll holder or something similar for the piston and connect a drive-shaft to a wheel. Technic Lego might be a useful aid. **Te**
- Ask the children to plan and build a bridge across a gap between two tables. These can be tested for weight-carrying ability. **Te**
- The children could add to their display pictures of transport in Victorian times. **Hi 1/4c**
- Discuss the paintings on pages 16 and 17 in the *Victorian Britain Group Discussion Book*.
- BLM 12 – Designing a railway advertisement.

Victorian medicine

Background information

At the start of the Victorian period the importance of clean water and living conditions was not fully realised. Amongst the filth and debris, diseases like cholera, typhoid fever and typhus flourished. Health care was rudimentary too. Doctors did not have to be qualified, there was no health service, and doctors had to be paid. Many dedicated doctors charged their rich patients high prices so that they could give free or cheap help to the poor. Average life expectancy was in the low 40s and only went up slightly in the whole of the period – infant mortality rates were especially high.

The most feared disease was cholera. A cholera attack is usually violent and kills suddenly. Over half the people who caught cholera died. It was not selective between rich and poor, though it did seem to spread amongst the poorest people in society more easily. Major epidemics came to Britain in 1831–32, 1848–49, 1854 and 1867. In the first part of the period doctors thought it just floated in the air. In 1848 Parliament heard that cholera was on its way. It set up the General Board of Health which collected evidence about the epidemic. Dr John Snow spent a lot of time investigating cholera and in 1855 he published a book that outlined how cholera could be spread within households and between households. Personal hygiene and a clean water supply seemed to prevent the spread of cholera.

At the start of Victoria's reign common treatments included the use of leeches and the use of hot irons to clean wounds. Surgery was appalling. Often no anaesthetics were used other than a bottle of brandy! During the period a whole range of discoveries and inventions made medical treatment a lot safer. The use of chloroform and of antiseptics meant that people were more likely to survive operations. Stethoscopes, thermometers and better microscopes all helped diagnosis. Vaccinations and the development of X-rays all helped in the prevention and cure of disease. Hospitals themselves changed dramatically thanks to the work of dedicated women like Florence Nightingale and Mary Seacole. (You can read more about Mary Seacole in the Ginn Key Stage 1 *Teachers' Handbook*.)

Looking at evidence

The following come from John Snow's book, *On the Mode of Communicating Cholera*, published in 1855: 'It is among the poor, where a whole family live, sleep, cook, eat and wash in a single room, that cholera has been found to spread when once introduced. When, on the other hand, cholera is introduced into the better kind of houses, it hardly ever spreads from one member of the family to another. The constant use of the handbasin and towel, and the fact of the places for cooking and eating being separate from the sick room, are the cause of this. The speed with which cholera spreads in institutions for pauper children confirms this. In the home for pauper children at Tooting, there were one hundred and forty deaths from cholera amongst a thousand inmates, and the disease did not cease until all the children had been removed.

If the cholera had no means of spreading, other than those which we have been considering, it would confine itself chiefly to the crowded dwellings of the poor, and would quickly die out for want of the chance to reach fresh victims: but there is another way open to it to spread itself more widely, and to reach the well-to-do classes of the community. I refer to the mixture of the cholera evacuations with the water used for drinking.'

Discussion and activities

- Read or give the children the evidence from John Snow's book, and ask them how they would avoid catching cholera if they lived in 1855. What would they do to lessen the risks? **Hi 3/3, 4**
- Ask the children to use the evidence from these pages to explain why people were living longer by the end of the century. **Hi 1/3b, 3/3**
- Discuss the pictures on page 20 in the *Victorian Britain Group Discussion Book*.
- BLM 14 – Designing a poster warning people of the dangers of cholera.

Art and literature

Background information

Charles Dickens (1812-70)

Charles Dickens published *Oliver Twist* in the year that Victoria came to the throne (1837). He was an outstandingly popular novelist of his time and has remained so. His books often revolve around characters who have money problems. This may be a reflection of his own childhood. His books appeared in instalments at first, as Dickens established himself. They present a remarkable comment on social life in the earlier part of Victoria's reign. Dickens' work often helped focus attention on the poor.

Lewis Carroll (1832-98)

Lewis Carroll was actually a mathematician called C. L. Dodgson. Not only were his stories popular because of his sense of nonsense but they were popular with parents too because they had a moral.

Frances Hodgson Burnett (1849-24)

Frances Hodgson Burnett was born in Manchester, England. Her family emigrated to America in 1856. Initially she was a short-story writer for magazines. Although *A Little Princess* was not published as a novel until 1905 it was originally a very popular magazine serial. Her first novel was published in 1876.

Alfred, Lord Tennyson (1809-92)

Alfred Tennyson made little money from writing until when he was only 33 he was given a pension from the Civil List so that he could concentrate on his writing. He was made Poet Laureate in 1850.

William Turner (1775-1851)

William Turner was a great Victorian artist. He was immensely popular in his own time and exhibited regularly at the Royal Academy. When he died he left his pictures and sketches to the nation.

William Morris (1834-96)

William Morris was educated at Oxford University. We best remember him for his design work in wallpaper, fabrics, tapestry, tiles and stained glass. Morris was not just a designer, though. He was also a well-known poet and a keen socialist.

Artists

The distrust between the public and artists was mutual. Successful businessmen regarded artists as charlatans who demanded high prices for something that did not seem like hard, honest work. The artists on the other hand liked to shock the bourgeoisie. Artists began to see themselves as a group apart and gradually during the period took on long hair and beards, velvet or corduroy clothes and wide-brimmed hats. On the other hand all middle- and upper-class homes would have had a number of pictures hanging on their walls.

Museums and galleries

Most of the great museums of Britain were founded in the Victorian times. By the end of the century nearly every major city had its own museum and art gallery. These were a sign of the importance of the city and were often impressive buildings in their own right.

Discussion and activities

- Ask the children to find as many books by Victorian novelists as they can. They can then read them, review them and see what they tell us about Victorian life. How do the novel's pictures compare with the pictures in the *Pupils' Book*?

- The children's own display work, or their own books on the Victorians, can be mounted or covered with Morris wallpaper. The children could try to devise their own Victorian designs.

38/39

Entertainment and leisure

Background information

At the beginning of the period people of the working class spent at least 10 hours a day at work and had little money. They spent their evenings at home or in a local pub. In the pub, for a penny, they could get drunk and forget their miserable living conditions. Their only holidays were Christmas Day, Good Friday and Sundays. As the century progressed, working hours became shorter and some employers allowed workers an afternoon off (Saturday usually) or even an unpaid annual holiday.

Sports

With more leisure time the middle classes became engaged in a variety of active sports. They might have tennis parties, or cycle, or play cricket and football. The working classes also played football. Some of our present-day football clubs can trace their origins back to the Victorian period – Arsenal, Everton and Blackburn Rovers were some of the top clubs at the time.

Music halls

Music halls were probably the most popular form of entertainment. Singers, magicians, trapeze artists and comedians entertained both rich and poor. Marie Lloyd's most famous song begins, 'My old man said follow the van, and don't dilly dally on the way'.

Seaside resorts

As there was more leisure time and the railways made travelling cheaper, more and more people took seaside holidays. Ideas about bathing were fairly mixed, as the extract from *Kilvert's Diary* on page 19 shows.

Looking at evidence

This is how Henry Mayhew described the leisure of the poor: 'Their leisure is devoted to the beer-house; the dancing room and the theatre. Home has few attractions. Skittles is a favourite amusement; the game is always for beer, but betting goes on. A fondness for sparring and boxing lingers among the rough members of some classes. "Twopenny hops" are much resorted to by the costermongers, men and women, boys and girls. The numbers present at these hops vary from thirty to one hundred of both sexes, their ages being from fourteen to forty-five. There is nothing of the leisurely style of dancing – half a glide and half a skip – but vigorous and laborious capering. The hours are from half-past eight to twelve, sometimes to one or two in the morning, and never later than two, as the costermongers are early risers. The other amusements of this class of the community are the theatre and the penny concert, and their visits are almost entirely confined to the galleries of the theatres on the Surrey-side . . . Among the men, rat killing is a favourite sport. They will enter an old stable, fasten the door, and then turn out the rats. Or they will find some unfrequented yard, and at night time build up a pit with apple-case boards, and lighting their lamps, enjoy the sport. Nearly every coster is fond of dogs. Some fancy them greatly and are proud of making them fight. Their dog fights are both cruel and frequent.'

This is what happened to Francis Kilvert when he went swimming at Seaton in Devon: 'A boy brought me to the machine door two towels as I thought, but when I came out of the water and began to use them I found that one of the rags he had given me was a pair of very short red and white striped drawers to cover my nakedness. Unaccustomed to such things and customs I had in my ignorance bathed naked and set at naught the conventionalities of the place and scandalized the beach. However, some little boys who were looking on at the rude naked man appeared to be much interested in the spectacle, and the young ladies who were strolling near seemed to have no objection.'

Discussion and activities

* Read Henry Mayhew's account of leisure to the children. Using this evidence and that in the *Pupils' Book*, they should make pictures to show leisure activities of the poor. **Hi 3/3, 4**
* Some children will enjoy writing to local football clubs to see if they have Victorian origins. **En 3**
* Read the children Kilvert's embarrassing moment. What can the children decide about bathing in the sea from this? **Hi 3/3**
* Discuss the seaside pictures on page 21 in the *Victorian Britain Group Discussion Book*.

Religion and the Victorian Sunday

Background information

The church

We have a notion that all Victorians went to church. A survey in 1851 showed that only about a third of the population attended church or chapel; this number probably rose to about half as the century progressed. The upper classes mainly attended the Church of England but Baptist and Methodist chapels were popular for middle- and working-class people. For many people, attendance at church on a Sunday was as much a social duty as a religious one. The same could be said of some of the clergy. Some clergymen were sons of the lesser gentry, and many of them seemed less interested in religion than in the social life and promotion. However, there were also many hard-working clergy in the towns and the country.

Sundays

Sunday was the family day. In many homes the day would start with a prayer or a reading by members of the family. Then church would be attended, sometimes twice. The type of service now as then would depend on the denomination; you could be sure it would be long! After church, families might walk together in the park. Children might be allowed to play but only with toys that had religious significance like Noah's Ark.

Life was very different for the poor. Few of them went to church, preferring to spend their time resting after a hard week's work. Much of their time would be spent in the pub. Sunday observance laws, now as then, created a good deal of feeling.

Christmas

The first Christmas card was invented in 1843 by Henry Cole and designed by J. C. Horsley. It showed a family dinner with three generations present. There was no tree, of course, because the tree was a German custom, only introduced later (1848) by Prince Albert to the Royal Family.

Looking at evidence

Molly Vivian Hughes wrote the following in her book *A London Child of the Seventies*: 'My back still aches in memory of those long services. Nothing was spared us. The seats and kneeling boards were constructed for grown-ups (and not too comfortable for them), and a child had the greatest difficulty in keeping an upright kneeling position all through the long intoned Litany.'

Discussion and activities

* Ask the children to design their own Christmas cards with a Victorian theme.
* Get the children to conduct a survey about what they do at the weekend. **Ma 5/4b**
* Discuss the painting on page 22 in the *Victorian Britain Group Discussion Book*.

Government, law and punishment

Background information

Disraeli and Gladstone

Benjamin Disraeli and William Gladstone dominated the Victorian political scene for a great part of the period. Between them they were Chancellor of the Exchequer or Prime Minister for much of the period between 1852 and 1894:

1852	Chancellor	Disraeli
1852–58	Chancellor	Gladstone
1858	Chancellor	Disraeli
1859–65	Chancellor	Gladstone
1866–68	Chancellor	Disraeli
1868	Prime Minister	Disraeli
1868–74	Prime Minister	Gladstone
1874–80	Prime Minister	Disraeli
1880–85	Prime Minister	Gladstone
1886	Prime Minister	Gladstone
1892–1894	Prime Minister	Gladstone

Disraeli died in 1881 and Gladstone in 1898. Disraeli was made Earl of Beaconsfield in 1876. Most of Victoria's prime ministers were in the House of Lords.

Parliamentary reform

The 1867 Reform Act gave the vote to all the male householders and men paying rent of at least £10 a year. In the country, men owning land rated at least at £54 a year or paying £12 a year rent were also given the vote. The constituencies were reformed as well so that some of the smaller areas lost one MP and the bigger cities gained MPs. The 1884–85 reforms gave countrymen the same rights as townsmen. The smaller areas lost all their MPs and larger towns were given more. No longer could the rich landowner be returned to Parliament by members of his family!

The police

The police force wore blue uniforms and top hats (later replaced by helmets) to show that they were not soldiers. They carried truncheons instead of guns. The first police force was in London, but by the 1850s most towns and cities had their own forces. Many of the largest cities had areas where even the police would not go except in large numbers. Gradually the cities and towns were made safer.

Punishment

Punishments for crimes were very severe, and included flogging, imprisonment, transportation and hanging. Transportations ended in 1867. A hanging was regarded as a great public spectacle. In early Victorian gaols prisoners were crammed together and were often beaten and starved by their gaolers. Gaolers were unpaid so had to make money any way they could – at the prisoners' expense! Later reforms made prisons better places but in some prisons prisoners were not allowed to talk and in others they were made to live in solitary confinement. Gaolers were replaced by paid warders, and prisoners could have their sentence reduced by good behaviour.

Looking at evidence

One individual, Thomas Miller, had been to prison five times by the time he was 12 and had been flogged twice.

Disraeli was very concerned at the divide between rich and poor. He described Britain as: 'two nations, between whom there is no contact and no sympathy; we are as ignorant of each other's habits, thoughts and feelings, as if we were dwellers in different zones, or inhabitants of different planets.'

Discussion and activities

- Read Disraeli's words to the children. What do they think he meant by them? Is this a fact or a viewpoint? Using the evidence from the rest of the book, do they agree or disagree with him? **Hi 2/3**
- Ask the children what they know of Sherlock Holmes. Was he real or fictional? More ghoulish class members can find out about Jack the Ripper.
- Discuss the picture of a treadmill on page 23 in the *Victorian Britain Group Discussion Book*.
- BLM 16 – Looking at Victorian reforms.

The British Empire

Background information

By the end of Victoria's reign Britain was the centre of a huge empire. At the start of her reign Britain already controlled Australia, Canada and New Zealand. Most of the African states were added during the 19th century. The British Empire also included parts of the Far East, the Caribbean and Pacific and Indian Ocean islands. Australia, Canada and New Zealand were the focus for many people who left Britain. In times of recession or when rural life became hard, many people emigrated to these countries. Australia had many prisoners transported to it until the 1840s. In these countries local customs were often ignored and the local people were often treated badly. In Australia the Aborigines and in New Zealand the Maoris were treated so harshly that at one time it seemed as if their way of life would be totally destroyed. It was the power of the British navy and army that made this great empire so big.

The countries of the empire supplied a whole host of cheap goods for the British market:

Australia	wool, mutton and gold
India	silk, tea and cotton
New Zealand	wool and mutton
Canada	timber, wheat and beef
African colonies – including Gambia, Gold Coast (Ghana), Nigeria, Kenya, Sudan, Egypt, Uganda, Rhodesia (Zimbabwe), South Africa	gold, diamonds, cocoa, coffee and timber

Discussion and activities

- Discuss with the children why people wanted an empire. Who do they think had the best reasons? How do the children think the original inhabitants felt about being 'taken over'? **Hi 1/2b, 3b, 4b, 5b**
- Discuss the map of the British Empire on page 24 in the *Victorian Britain Group Discussion Book*.

Victorian heritage

These pages deliberately focus on things that might be seen locally which link the Victorians with the present. Further ideas on local studies are given on pages 24–26.

Discussion and activities

- **BLM 17** – Distinguishing between early and late Victorian events.
- **BLM 18** – Constructing a Victorian time line.
- **BLM 19** – Finding out about famous Victorian people.

Key *Victorian Britain* events

Date	Event
1837	Victoria becomes Queen, when she is just 18 years old.
1840	Queen Victoria and Prince Albert marry.
1840	The first national postal service is introduced.
1842	The Mines Act stops children under 10 working in the mines.
1844	The Factory Act stops children between 8 and 13 working more than 6½ hours a day.
1845–47	Irish famine results in large-scale emigration from Ireland.
1847	The Ten Hours Act stops women, and children under 18, working more than 10 hours a day.
1848	The first Christmas tree is introduced to Britain by Prince Albert.
1848	The Public Health Act is passed to try to make large towns healthier places.
1851	The Great Exhibition is opened at Crystal Palace by Prince Albert.
1853–56	The Crimean War.
1857	The Indian War of Independence.
1858	The telegraph system is established between England and the United States.
1859	Charles Darwin's book, on the *Origin of Species,* is published.
1861	Prince Albert dies of typhoid.
1861	Mrs Beeton's book *Household Management,* is published.
1863	The first underground railway, the Metropolitan Line, is opened in London.
1867	The right to vote is widened to include most men.
1870	Education Act is passed. Boards of Education are set up to provide schooling in every area.
1872	Secret ballots are established.
1873	The Great Agricultural Depression.
1876	Alexander Bell invents the telephone.
1880	The Education Act makes schooling compulsory for all children between 5 and 10.
1901	Queen Victoria dies. Her son, Edward VII, succeeds.

Further references

Non-fiction

There is a wealth of non-fiction books about the Victorians, but they do not always match the National Curriculum.

- [ ] E. Allan, *Victorian Children*, A & C Black.
- [ ] L. Chaney, *Breakfast*, A & C Black, 1990.
- [ ] D. Evans, *How We Used to Live, Victorians Early and Late*, A & C Black, 1990.
- [ ] R. Hart, *English Life in the Nineteenth Century*, Wayland, 1971.
- [ ] J. Hook, *Stephenson and the Industrial Revolution*, Wayland, 1987.
- [ ] S. Purkis, *At Home and in the Street in 1900*, Longman, 1981.
- [ ] S. Purkis, *At School and in the Country in 1900*, Longman, 1981.
- [ ] M. Stoppleman, *School Day*, A & C Black, 1990.
- [ ] R. Thompson, *In the Post*, A & C Black, 1990.
- [ ] R. Thompson, *Washday*, A & C Black, 1990.
- [ ] T. Triggs, *Victorian Britain*, Wayland, 1990.
- [ ] R. Unstead, *Age of Machines*, Macdonald, 1974.

Fiction

There is a wealth of Victorian fiction, but it makes most sense to read the most popular fiction written in the period, especially:

- [ ] Charles Dickens, *Oliver Twist*, Penguin Classics, 1985.
- [ ] Charles Dickens, *Nicholas Nickleby*, Penguin Classics, 1978.
- [ ] Charles Dickens, *A Christmas Carol*, Puffin Classics, 1985.
- [ ] Lewis Carroll, *Alice's Adventures in Wonderland*, Puffin Classics, 1985.
- [ ] Frances Hodgson Burnett, *A Little Princess*, Puffin Classics, 1951.
- [ ] Frances Hodgson Burnett, *The Secret Garden*, Puffin Classics, 1951.
- [ ] Frances Hodgson Burnett, *Little Lord Fauntleroy*, Puffin Classics, 1951.

Television

- [ ] *How We Used to Live*, Yorkshire Television, has a tremendous impact on children but should be used carefully with the teachers' notes.
- [ ] Some of the *Landmarks* programmes are of use.

Places of interest

There are many interesting visits that can be made when studying the Victorians. Some of these are:

- [ ] Abbey House Museum, Kirkstall, Leeds. A walk-around living museum.
- [ ] Beamish Open Air Museum, Beamish, County Durham. Period reconstruction of Beamish village.
- [ ] Bedford Museum, Bedford. An excellent series of rooms furnished as a Victorian middle-class home.
- [ ] Blists Hill Museum, Ironbridge Gorge, Telford. A living museum of a small community with houses, shops and an inn.
- [ ] Castle Museum, York. Contains a Victorian street.
- [ ] Cambridge and County Folk Museum, Cambridge. Victorian rural life.
- [ ] Morwhellan Quay, Nr Tavistock, Devon. An open-air museum of a small copper-mining community.
- [ ] The Museum of Childhood, Bethnal Green, London. Contains a good collection of Victorian toys and dolls.
- [ ] The Museum of Childhood, Edinburgh. Collections include Victorian toys.
- [ ] The Museum of Childhood, Sudbury, Derbyshire. This museum shows how children lived in the period.
- [ ] The Victoria and Albert Museum, London. Good collections of costume and furniture.

There are a number of places related to Charles Dickens. Some of these are:

- [ ] Dickens House Museum, Broadstairs, Kent.
- [ ] The Dickens House Museum, Doughty Street, London.
- [ ] The Charles Dickens Centre, Rochester, Kent.

Local history study

The supplementary study unit for local history may be used to study an aspect of the local community that illustrates developments taught in other study units. Local history work could therefore be used to complement the work being carried out on the Victorians.

There is a range of resources available for a local history study. The most important resource has to be the local area itself. Visits will need to be arranged for the class. During a visit, plenty of photographs should be taken.

The local history library or record office are important centres for documentary sources. A whole range of sources should be available including the following:

- Maps of your area. The comparison of large-scale maps over a number of years can be very revealing. Children are often struck by the massive change that has occurred in some areas over the last 100 years. Different scales can be a problem but the careful use of transparencies and the OHP can remedy this.
- Census returns. These are available for much of the Victorian era and provide a great deal of statistical information about families and occupations in the period. It is relatively simple to obtain these for a street in the area and then you can match real families to real houses. The use of data-handling packages such as Grass or Quest enable children to make a variety of investigations from a large body of statistics.
- Directories. These were printed for many areas between 1830 and 1930 and give a clear picture of the make-up of a local community. Changing patterns of population and occupation can be traced. For instance, it is possible to determine how the use of a particular row of shops has changed over a period.
- Old photographs and postcard collections. These can be a rich source on which to base investigations about change or to investigate the later part of the 19th and the earlier part of the 20th century.

There is a range of other sources which can be very productive but they are initially more time consuming to use: for example local newspapers, inventories, parish records, quarter sessions and poor relief documents. The local history librarian may be able to give you guidance. Local teachers' centres, urban studies centres or advisers may also have relevant collections.

Although the collection of material is time consuming, once collected it will provide a resource for a considerable time.

Example of a local history study

Key issues	Concepts	Content	Sources	Activities	Teaching and learning methods	Assessment questions	Cross-curricular links
• Do Victorian houses and buildings still exist?	• Continuity and change	• Victorian houses in locality	• Local row of houses/shops • Old photographs	• Observational drawing • Listing similarities and differences	• Fieldwork • Discussion • Individual written work	• How are the houses different to houses now? • What alterations might have been made since the houses were built? AT 1/3a, 3b, 4a, 4b	Ar En
• Who lived in those houses? • What do we know about them?	• Evidence • Census • Family relationships • Occupations	• The occupants of local houses in the Victorian period	• Census material, preferably transcribed onto card – one card per household	• In pairs children should describe the original occupants of houses to each other. • Children should each select a household, and research and collect materials about the family. They could compile a book about the family, which may include a family tree.	• Discussion • Familiarisation with source material • Investigation of sources in small groups or pairs	• How do we know? AT 3	En
• What work did the Victorians do?	• Paid employment • Unpaid work • Scholars • Continuity and change	• Local Victorian occupations	• Census • Library books • Dictionary	• Children should write a description of the jobs that members of their Victorian family did.	• Small group or period research	• How do we know what the jobs are? AT 3 • Are there jobs like that now? AT 1/3a, 4a • What did the people with no recorded occupation do? AT 2/4	En Gg

Example of a local history study (continued)

Key issues	Concepts	Content	Sources	Activities	Teaching and learning methods	Assessment questions	Cross-curricular links
• Who lived in those houses? • What don't we know about them?	• Evidence • Secondary sources	• What did the people look like? What did they wear, eat, etc? • How was their home furnished?	• *Ginn Pupils' Book – Victorian Britain* • Portraits • Old photographs	• Investigate 'typical' clothing and furnishings of the Victorians at the date of census. • Writing and artwork	• Small group or paired research	• How do we know? • Are they really like that? AT 3	En
• What did the Victorian children do?	• Education • Leisure • Toys	• Schooling • Toys and games • School log book	• *Ginn Pupils' Book* • Library books	• Children should compare their typical day with that of a Victorian child	• Small group or paired investigation	• How do we know? AT 3	En
• What new things might your family have?	• Inventions	• Victorian inventions, lighting communication, etc.	• *Ginn Pupils' Book* and other secondary sources	• Children should add illustrations and captions to their own books.	• Small group or paired investigation		
• How settled was Victorian life? • How long did people live in their house?	• Migration, internal and external	• Matching families from census to those on directory • Length of stay • Birthplaces	• Census • Directories • Atlases • Local maps	• Comparing the directory and census • List the birthplaces and find them on a map.	• Research using census and directory • Small group research (using map indexes)	• How do we know? • What is your evidence? AT 3 • How do we know? • Why do you think they were/were not born here? AT 2, 3	Gg
• What changes have happened to the area since your family lived here?	• Change	• Changes over time in the locality	• Maps • Photographs	• Write about changes the Victorian family would notice now.	• Small group research	• What makes you think they would notice that? • Why do you think it has changed?	En, Gg
• Looking closer at the family's home		• What did the house look like originally?	• Local houses, etc.	• Revisit observational drawings. Work into finish artwork or model.	• Fieldwork • Art or technology work		Ar, Te
		• Final touches to own book	• Results from own research • Computer	• Children should record their information on a computer, and put all their research on their Victorian family into a book.	• Individual and small group work	AT 1/4c	En, Te

Blackline Masters

The Blackline Masters extend themes developed in the *Pupils' Book*. They also provide additional forms of evidence to examine. The BLMs therefore encourage children to go back and re-examine the *Pupils' Book,* practise their information book skills, and to read with a purpose.

On each sheet the key skill or concept that the BLM develops is marked at the top. A full explanation of these key skills, and how they can be used as an ideal aid to assessment and record-keeping, can be found in the Key Stage 2 *Teachers' Handbook.*

Symbols are given at the top of some BLMs:

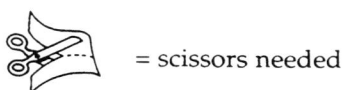

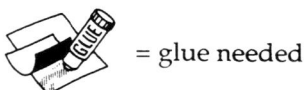

= scissors needed

= glue needed

The table below indicates the following:

- Which Blackline Master relates to each *Victorian Britain Pupils' Book* page.
- Which Blackline Master resources different historical perspectives (political/ economic, technological and scientific/ social/ religious/ cultural and aesthetic).
- Which Blackline Master resources aspects of the thematic supplementary study units.

(Valuable time-saving charts showing how *Victorian Britain* can be linked with the supplementary study units can be found in the Key Stage 2 *Teachers' Handbook.*)

Perspective/theme	Pupils' Book page																						
	2	4	6	8	10	12	14	16	18	20	22	24	26	28	30	32	34	36	38	40	42	44	46
Political								16	16	16											16		
Economic, technical and scientific														19			14, 19						
Social						3,5	4,5			10			10										
Religious																							
Cultural and aesthetic																							
Ships and seafarers																							
Food and farming																							
Houses and places of worship					6	6	4,6																
Writing and printing										11													
Land transport															13	12, 13							
Domestic life, families and childhood	1	2, 19	8			3, 8, 15	4	8	7, 8	9, 11											12		

Victorian Britain

The air and the soil appear charged with fog and soot. Manufactories with their blackened bricks, their naked fronts, their windows destitute of shutters, and resembling huge and cheap penitentiaries.

Taine

Manchester is the most wonderful city of modern times. It is the philosopher alone who can conceive the grandeur of Manchester and the immensity of its future.

. . . dirt and revolting filth – without qualification the most horrible dwelling I have until now beheld.

Engels

Disraeli

Why do you think these visitors held such different views of Manchester?
Describe the features that would impress you in a Victorian city.
Describe the features that you would dislike.

Compare your point of view with a friend's.

BLM
1

Victorian Britain

Complete this water diary, showing when you use water during the day.

Morning	Afternoon	Evening
Brushing teeth	Drink of orange juice	Cooking vegetables

Cut out the entries from your water diary, and arrange them in order of priority, beginning with the most important.

Imagine that you are living in Frying Pan Alley, a Victorian slum street. The water is only on for 20 minutes each day. Which activities would you use the water for?

_____

_____

_____

What were some of the effects of not having an adequate supply of clean water in Victorian times?

_____

_____

_____

Victorian Britain

Rich Victorian families had a number of servants who lived and worked in their homes. What did each of these servants do?

Butler

_____

_____

_____

_____

Chambermaid

_____

_____

_____

_____

Parlourmaid

_____

_____

_____

_____

Gardener

_____

_____

_____

_____

Cook

_____

_____

_____

_____

Nanny

_____

_____

_____

_____

Imagine that you are a rich Victorian who needs another servant.
Write a newspaper advertisement for the servant.
What will the servant be expected to do?

Victorian Britain

You have visited the local workhouse, and are shocked by some of the conditions that you have seen. Write a letter to the workhouse Board of Guardians stating some of your concerns, and making some suggestions for improvements.

The Firs
Sheffield

October 9th 1876

To The Board of Guardians

Dear Sir,

Why do you think life in the workhouse was so harsh?

Victorian Britain

... two nations, between whom there is no contact and no sympathy; we are as ignorant of each other's habits, thoughts and feelings, as if we were dwellers in different zones, or inhabitants of different planets.

This is what Benjamin Disraeli, a Victorian prime minister said. Do you think this is a good description of the contrast between wealthy and poor families in Victorian times? Use the chart to write down differences between Victorian families which you have noticed.

Wealthy Victorian families	Poor Victorian families

Victorian Britain

Change and continuity
Cause and effect

Complete this inventory of the contents of your home.

My home

beds	television	carpet
chairs	pictures	_____
armchairs	lamps	_____
cooker	wardrobe	_____

Use the pictures on pages 10 and 11 in the *Pupils' Book* to help you to complete inventories for rich and poor Victorian families' homes.

A rich family's home

A poor family's home

Compare the inventories, and suggest reasons for the differences.

© Ginn and Company Ltd 1992. Copying permitted by purchasing school only. This material is not copyright free.

BLM
6

Victorian Britain

Politician trying to stop the use of climbing boys

Poor family

Chimney sweep

Wealthy home owner

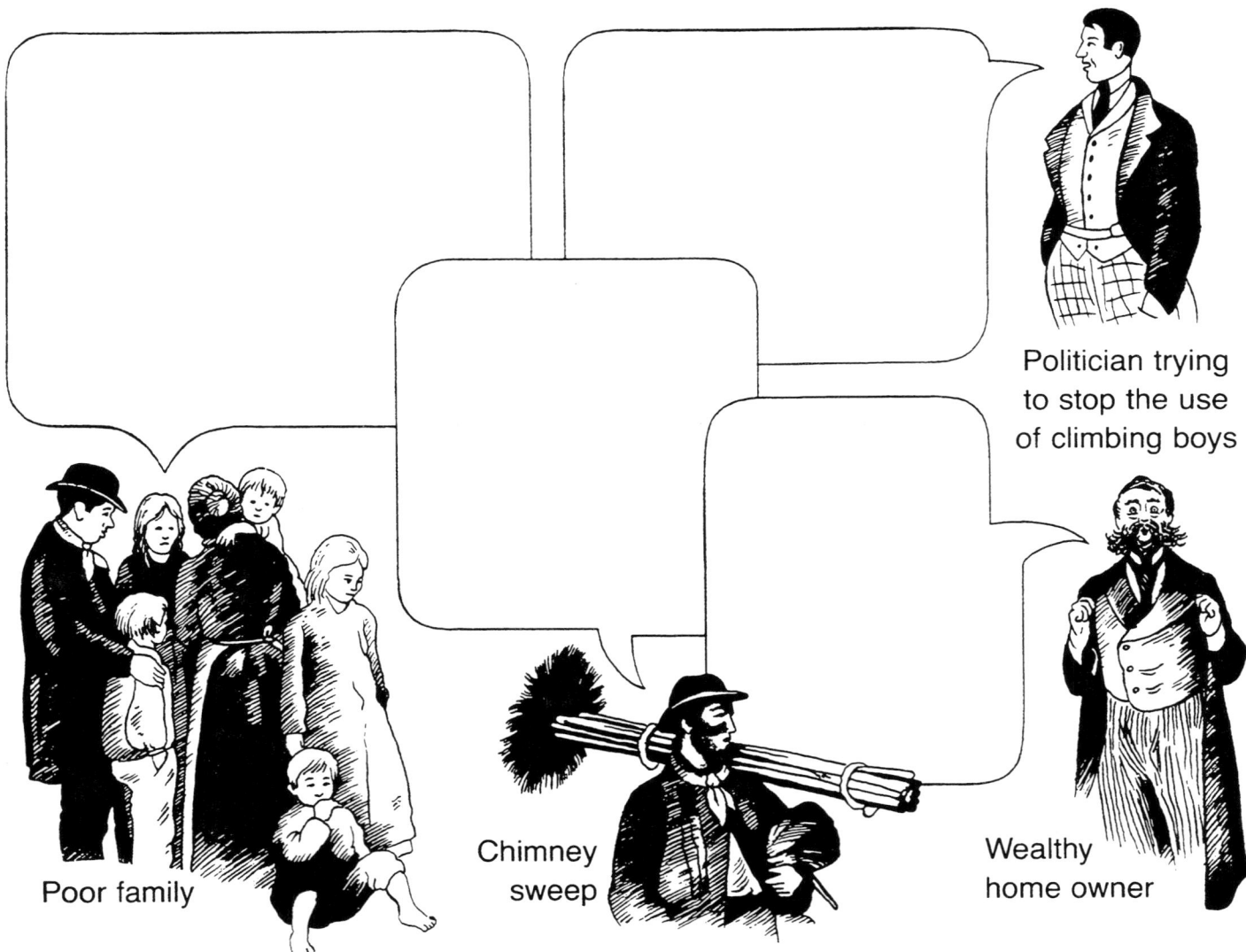

Write in the speech bubbles what these people might have said about the employment of climbing boys. Are your comments fact or opinion?

Imagine that you are a climbing boy talking to a politician about your job. How would you describe the dangers of your job?

_____

_____

_____

_____

_____

Victorian Britain

Write a description of each of the following Victorian worker's jobs.

1. _____

_____

_____

_____

2. _____

_____

_____

_____

3. _____

_____

_____

_____

4. _____

_____

_____

_____

Victorian Britain

5. _____

_____

_____

_____

6. _____

_____

_____

_____

If you lived in Victorian times, which of these jobs would you have chosen and why?

_____

_____

Some of these jobs do not exist now. Fill in this table telling which jobs still exist. If the jobs do not exist, explain why not.

Job description	Does it still exist?	If not, why not?
Coal miner		
School teacher		
Chimney sweep		
Lamplighter		
Street trader		
Factory worker		
'Bearer' in a coal mine		
Governess		
Washerwoman		

Grindle Board School – 1882

a.m.

9.15-9.30	*Registration. Examination of hands and shoes. Prayers*
9.30-9.45	*Tables by rote*
9.45-10.30	*Arithmetic*
10.30-10.45	*Playtime*
10.45-11.15	*Religious instruction and Bible story*
11.15-11.45	*Handwriting*
11.45-12.00	*Spelling*
12.00-1.15	*Lunchtime*

p.m.

1.15-2.15	*Needlework for girls* *Woodwork for boys*
2.15-2.45	*Drill in the playground*
2.45-3.00	*Playtime*
3.00-3.30	*Poetry recitation. Story. Prayers*

Compare this Victorian timetable with your own daily school timetable.
Are there any similarities?

My school timetable

BLM
9

Victorian Britain

The aim of education is to fit children for the position in life which they are hereafter to occupy . . . girls are to dwell in quiet homes, amongst a few friends.

Elizabeth Sewell, 1866

Parents who have daughters will always look to their being provided for in marriage, will always believe that the gentler graces and winning qualities of character will be their best passports to marriage and will always expect their husbands to take on themselves the intellectual toil and active exertions needed for the support of the family.

Report of Schools Inquiry Commission, 1867-68

. . . medical men said there was not the same physical power and strength in the fibres of the brain as would enable the majority of girls to compete with each other in the high branches of mathematics and other subjects of that kind requiring great mental power and attention.

Lord Hatherley, quoted in the *Journal of Women's Education Union,* 1876

In Victorian times, people had differing views about the education of girls. What do you think? Write lists of the reasons why girls should be educated, and the reasons against educating girls.

Victorian Britain

Victorian people thought good handwriting was very important. At school, children practised handwriting for many hours each week. Children wrote with pens dipped in ink on copybooks. First they wrote over an outline and then they wrote the letters below. The phrases they copied taught the children good behaviour.

Use pen and ink to complete this page from a copybook.

Spare the rod, spoil the child

Neglect no opportunity of doing good

Spare the brush, spoil the teeth

Remember not to blot your copybook!

Victorian Britain

Design a railway advertisement to attract visitors to a Victorian seaside resort. What attractions does the resort have for visitors?

Victorian Britain

Cut out the pictures and stick them on a time line, to show how transport changed during Victorian times.

Add your own pictures of transport to the time line.

In what ways were people's lives affected by improved means of transport?

BLM
13

Victorian Britain

Design a poster, warning of the dangers of cholera and suggesting precautions which could be taken to avoid the disease.

Remember that not all Victorian people could read!

Victorian Britain

Family portraits became increasingly popular in late Victorian times. Draw your own family group, as it may have looked in Victorian times.

Victorian Britain

Many Victorian reforms affect our lives today.

Describe the reforms which led to:

better working conditions

_____

_____

_____

improved public health

_____

_____

_____

greater participation in government

_____

_____

_____

improved public order

_____

_____

_____

a more educated population

_____

_____

_____

Victorian Britain

These pictures show features of life in early and late Victorian times.
Cut out the pictures and arrange them according to whether you think they
belong to early or late Victorian times. Some pictures may belong to both periods.
Add your own pictures or writing about other early or late Victorian features.

Victorian Britain

Colour in the decades. Add further information to the time line as you learn about the Victorians.

1837
Victoria is crowned Queen

1840
Victoria and Albert marry

1851
The Great Exhibition

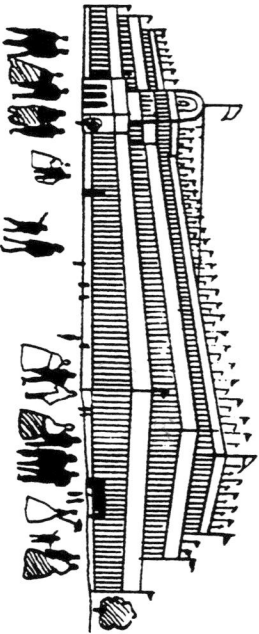

1855
Florence Nightingale and Mary Seacole work in the Crimea

1861
Prince Albert dies of typhoid fever

1876
Alexander Bell invents the telephone

1880
Education Act

1901
Queen Victoria dies – Edward VII becomes King

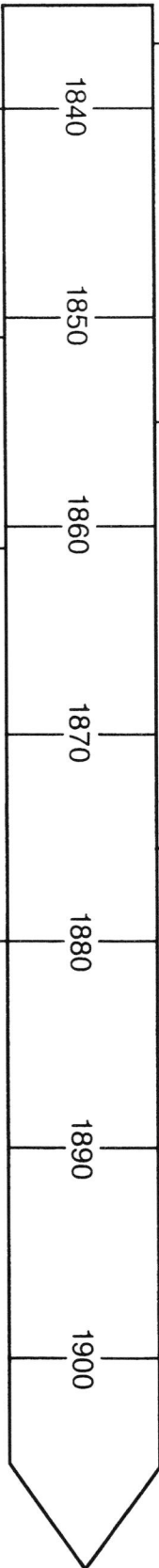

1840
1850
1860
1870
1880
1890
1900

Victorian Britain

Why are the following Victorian people famous?

Joseph Lister

Joseph Lister was a scientist who invented a disinfectant spray used in operations to stop people catching infections.

Charles Darwin

_____
_____
_____
_____
_____

Dr Barnardo

_____
_____
_____
_____

James Simpson

_____
_____
_____
_____

Alexander Bell

_____
_____
_____
_____

Mary Seacole

_____
_____
_____
_____

Louis Pasteur

_____
_____
_____
_____

William Booth

_____
_____
_____
_____

Victorian Britain

Find out more about one of these people by looking in books in the library.
Find out about, and make notes on, the following:

1. Born_____ Died_____

2. Main events in their life

    _____

    _____

3. Main achievements

    _____

    _____

4. Other interesting facts

    _____

    _____

    _____

Now write a short description of their life and main achievements.

_____

_____

_____

_____

_____